# INDEX

# Page 11 - Chapter Five: Discipline

# Page 12 - Conclusion

**Written By: Tory Ricalis**
**Published by: Vas Rel**

# INDEX FUND INVESTING THE WARREN BUFFETT WAY: 5 STEPS TO COMPOUND YOUR WEALTH OVER TIME

## **Forward**

Investing in index funds has become increasingly popular over the years, and Warren Buffett's index fund strategy is one that has gained significant attention. Buffett's strategy is rooted in the principles of long-term investing, consistency, and discipline.

As we all know, investing can be daunting, and without a solid plan, it can be easy to make impulsive decisions that can lead to significant losses. That is why the first step to implementing Buffett's strategy is to start with a sound investment plan that aligns with your financial goals, risk tolerance, and time horizon. This plan will serve as a roadmap for your investment journey and help you stay on track even during market volatility.

The next step is to choose a low-cost index fund. Buffett recommends investing in a low-cost S&P 500 index fund, which provides broad exposure to the US stock market and is one of the most popular index funds globally. A low-cost index fund with low expense ratios and fees is essential as it allows you to keep more of your investment returns.

Investing regularly is also crucial to Buffett's index fund strategy. By investing a set amount each month or quarter, you can take advantage of dollar-cost averaging, which helps to reduce the impact of market fluctuations on your investment returns. Consistency in investing is the key to long-term wealth building, and it requires patience, discipline, and commitment.

Over time, your portfolio may become unbalanced due to market fluctuations, and rebalancing your portfolio is the next step to implementing Buffet's index fund strategy. Rebalancing helps you maintain your target allocation, manage risk, and capitalize on opportunities.

Finally, staying the course is perhaps the most important step in implementing Buffett's index fund strategy. Long-term investing requires patience and discipline. It is easy to get caught up in short-term market fluctuations and make impulsive decisions that can be detrimental to your investment returns. It is crucial to avoid the temptation to react to short-term market fluctuations and stick to your investment plan. Remember that compounding takes time, but it can have a powerful effect on your wealth over the long term.

Warren Buffett's index fund strategy is an excellent starting point for those looking to invest for the long term. The five steps outlined in this book, starting with a sound investment plan, choosing a low-cost index fund, investing regularly, rebalancing your portfolio periodically, and staying the course, are essential to building long-term wealth. The principles of consistency, patience, and discipline are key to Buffett's index fund strategy, and they are the traits that any successful long-term investor must have.

## Introduction

Warren Buffett is one of the most successful investors of all time, with a net worth of over $100 billion. He is known for his disciplined investment strategy and his ability to generate consistent returns over the long term. One of the key components of Buffett's strategy is his index fund strategy, which involves investing in low-cost, passively-managed index funds over the long term.

In this introduction, we will explore the five steps to implementing Warren Buffett's index fund strategy to compound your wealth over time. These steps are based on Buffett's philosophy of long-term investing, risk management, and consistency.

# STEP 1: START WITH A SOUND INVESTMENT PLAN

Before investing, it is important to create a plan that fits your financial goals, risk tolerance, and time horizon. This will help you stay on track during market volatility and reduce the urge to make impulsive decisions. Buffett has always stressed the importance of having a sound investment plan, and he has said that it is one of the keys to his success.

Your investment plan should take into account your long-term financial goals, such as retirement or saving for a down payment on a house. It should also consider your risk tolerance, or how much risk you are willing to take on in pursuit of higher returns. Your investment plan should be tailored to your individual circumstances, and it should be flexible enough to adapt to changes in your life or financial situation.

# STEP 2: CHOOSE A LOW-COST INDEX FUND

Once you have created your investment plan, it is time to choose an index fund. An index fund is a type of mutual fund that tracks a specific index, such as the S&P 500, which is a broad-based index of 500 large-cap stocks. Because index funds are passively managed, they have lower expenses and fees than actively managed funds, which are run by professional fund managers.

Buffett recommends investing in a low-cost S&P 500 index fund, which gives you exposure to a broad range of stocks and diversifies your portfolio. By investing in a low-cost index fund, you can take advantage of the long-term growth potential of the stock market while minimizing expenses and fees.

# STEP 3: INVEST REGULARLY

Consistency is key to long-term wealth building. Once you have chosen your index fund, it is important to invest regularly. Set up a regular investment plan, such as contributing a set amount each month or quarter, and stick to it. This will help you take advantage of dollar-cost averaging, which means buying more shares when prices are low and fewer shares when prices are high.

Investing regularly also helps you avoid the temptation to try to time the market, which is a risky and often unsuccessful strategy. Instead, focus on the long-term growth potential of the stock market and let compounding work its magic.

# STEP 4: REBALANCE YOUR PORTFOLIO PERIODICALLY

Over time, your portfolio may become unbalanced due to market fluctuations. For example, if stocks have a strong run, they may make up a larger portion of your portfolio than you originally intended. Rebalancing your portfolio helps you maintain your target allocation, manage risk, and capitalize on opportunities.

To rebalance your portfolio, you can either sell some of your over performing assets or buy more of your underperforming assets. This helps you maintain a balanced portfolio and ensures that you are not taking on too much risk in any one asset class or sector.

# STEP 5: STAY THE COURSE

Long-term investing requires patience and discipline. The stock market can be volatile in the short term, and it is easy to be tempted by the allure of quick profits. However, Buffett has always stressed the importance of staying the course and avoiding the temptation to react to short-term market fluctuations.

Remember, compounding takes time, but it can have a powerful effect on your wealth over the long term. In fact, the power of compounding is one of the key reasons why Warren Buffett has been able to achieve such remarkable success. By consistently reinvesting his earnings, he has been able to grow his wealth at an incredible rate over the course of several decades.

The power of compounding can be illustrated by a simple example. Suppose you invest $10,000 in an index fund that earns an average annual return of 8% over a period of 30 years. After 30 years, your investment would be worth over $100,000, even if you never added another dime to your investment. This is the power of compounding, and it is a key reason why investing in low-cost index funds over the long term is such a powerful wealth-building strategy.

# CHAPTER ONE: PLANNING

Warren Buffett's index fund strategy is a proven approach to building long-term wealth. By starting with a sound investment plan, choosing a low-cost index fund, investing regularly, rebalancing your portfolio periodically, and staying the course, you can take advantage of the power of compounding and achieve your financial goals over the long term. Whether you are just starting out as an investor or are looking to fine-tune your investment strategy, following these five steps can help you achieve success in the stock market.

**Start with a sound investment plan:**
Before investing, it is important to create a plan that fits your financial goals, risk tolerance, and time horizon. This will help you stay on track during market volatility and reduce the urge to make impulsive decisions. Warren Buffett has always stressed the importance of having a sound investment plan, and he has said that it is one of the keys to his success.

Buffett's investment plan is centered on a few key principles, including long-term thinking, value investing, and diversification. He believes that investors should focus on buying quality companies with strong fundamentals and a long-term track record of growth. He also believes in diversification, which means spreading your investments across a range of asset classes, sectors, and geographic regions to reduce the risk of loss.

**Invest in quality companies:**
Buffett is known for his value investing approach, which involves buying stocks that are undervalued by the market. He looks for companies that have strong fundamentals, a competitive advantage, and a long-term track record of growth. He believes that by investing in quality companies with a strong brand and loyal customer base, he can minimize the risk of loss and achieve superior returns over the long term.

Buffett is also a long-term investor, and he believes that investors should focus on holding stocks for many years, even decades. He has said that his favorite holding period is "forever," and he has held some of his investments, such as Coca-Cola and American Express, for over 30 years.

**Diversify your portfolio:**
In addition to investing in quality companies, Buffett also stresses the importance of diversification. He believes that by spreading your investments across a range of asset classes, sectors, and geographic regions, you can reduce the risk of loss and achieve more consistent returns over the long term.

Buffett's approach to diversification is to focus on a few key sectors and asset classes that he understands well, such as banking, insurance, and consumer goods. He also looks for opportunities in emerging markets, which he believes offer significant growth potential in the long term.

**Manage your risk:**
One of the keys to Warren Buffett's success is his disciplined approach to risk management. He believes that investors should focus on minimizing their downside risk, rather than trying to maximize their upside potential. He has said that "risk comes from not knowing what you're doing," and he emphasizes the importance of doing your homework and understanding the companies you are investing in. Buffett also believes in the importance of staying disciplined and avoiding impulsive decisions. He has said that the stock market is like a "voting machine" in the short term, but a "weighing machine" in the long term. This means that market volatility can cause short-term fluctuations in stock prices, but over the long term, the underlying fundamentals of the company will determine its value.

Warren Buffett's investment philosophy is centered on a few key principles, including long-term thinking, value investing, and diversification. He believes that investors should focus on buying quality companies with a long-term track record of growth, and that they should diversify their portfolio to reduce the risk of loss. He also emphasizes the importance of disciplined risk management and avoiding impulsive decisions. By following these principles, investors can achieve consistent returns over the long term and minimize the risk of loss.

# CHAPTER TWO: VALUE

Warren Buffett is one of the most successful investors in history, and his investment philosophy is widely studied and followed by many investors around the world. One of the key components of Buffett's investment strategy is his emphasis on low-cost index funds, which he believes are the best way for individual investors to build wealth over the long term.

Buffett's approach to investing in index funds is simple yet effective. He recommends that investors choose a low-cost index fund that tracks a broad market index, such as the S&P 500. By investing in an index fund, investors can gain exposure to a wide range of stocks and achieve diversification without having to pick individual stocks themselves.

The reason Buffett emphasizes low-cost index funds is that he believes that high fees can erode investment returns over time. In his famous letter to Berkshire Hathaway shareholders in 2016, Buffett wrote, "When trillions of dollars are managed by Wall Streeters charging high fees, it will usually be the managers who reap outsized profits, not the clients."

Here are some of the reasons why low-cost index funds are a smart choice for individual investors:

1. Low fees: The most obvious advantage of low-cost index funds is that they have lower fees than actively managed funds. Since index funds simply track a market index, they require less active management and research, which translates into lower expenses. By minimizing fees, investors can keep more of their investment returns.

2. Diversification: By investing in an index fund, investors can achieve instant diversification across a broad range of stocks. Since index funds track a market index, they hold a diversified portfolio of stocks, which helps to reduce risk and volatility.

3. Passive management: Unlike actively managed funds, index funds do not rely on a team of analysts to select individual stocks. Instead, index funds simply track a market index, which means that they are passively managed. This can be an advantage because passive management is typically associated with lower costs and lower turnover, which can lead to more consistent returns over time.

4. Easy to understand: Index funds are relatively simple to understand, which makes them a great choice for individual investors who are new to investing. Since index funds track a market index, investors do not need to have a deep understanding of individual companies or market trends in order to invest.

5.  Historical performance: Over the long term, index funds have historically outperformed many actively managed funds. According to a study by S&P Dow Jones Indices, 85% of large-cap funds underperformed the S&P 500 over the 10-year period ending December 31, 2016. This means that investors who simply invested in an S&P 500 index fund would have outperformed the majority of active fund managers.

Buffett's recommendation to invest in low-cost index funds is not a new idea, but it is one that has gained popularity in recent years as investors have become more aware of the impact of fees on investment returns. By investing in low-cost index funds, investors can achieve a diversified portfolio of stocks, minimize fees, and benefit from the power of compounding over the long term.

In fact, Buffett himself has put his money where his mouth is when it comes to index funds. In 2007, he bet $1 million that an S&P 500 index fund would outperform a selection of hedge funds over a 10-year period. By 2017, the index fund had gained 85.4%, while the hedge funds had gained only 22%. This bet highlighted the power of index funds and the benefits of investing in a diversified portfolio of stocks over the long term.

It's worth noting that while Buffett recommends investing in a low-cost S&P 500 index fund, there are many other index funds available that may be suitable for individual investors. Ultimately, the best index fund for you will depend on your individual investment goals, risk tolerance, and financial situation. Some investors may prefer to invest in funds that track specific sectors or industries, while others may want exposure to international markets or small-cap stocks.

# CHAPTER THREE: RESEARCH

Before investing in any index fund, it's important to carefully research and compare different options to find the one that's right for you. Look at factors such as expense ratios, tracking error, diversification, and historical performance, and consider consulting with a financial advisor if you're unsure which fund is best for your needs.

In addition to the S&P 500 index fund, Buffett has also spoken favorably of other low-cost index funds, including those that track the total U.S. stock market or bond market. He has also recommended that investors avoid high-cost mutual funds that charge steep management fees and underperform the market over the long term.

Ultimately, the key to successful index fund investing is to focus on the long-term and avoid making impulsive decisions based on short-term market fluctuations. By staying disciplined, patient, and committed to a sound investment plan, individual investors can use index funds to build wealth and achieve their financial goals over time.

Investing regularly and consistently is a cornerstone of Warren Buffett's long-term approach to building wealth through index fund investing. By setting up a regular investment plan and sticking to it, individual investors can take advantage of a powerful strategy called dollar-cost averaging, which can help them reduce the impact of market fluctuations and maximize their returns over time.

Dollar-cost averaging is a simple but effective strategy that involves investing a fixed amount of money into an asset at regular intervals, regardless of the asset's price at the time. By investing a fixed amount on a regular basis, investors buy more shares when prices are low and fewer shares when prices are high, which can help smooth out the impact of market volatility and reduce the overall cost of investing. For example, suppose an investor sets up a regular investment plan to invest $1,000 in an index fund every month. If the index fund is trading at $100 per share, the investor will buy 10 shares that month. If the next month the index fund has fallen to $80 per share, the investor will buy 12.5 shares with the same $1,000 investment. By doing so, the investor has effectively bought more shares when the price was lower, which can help increase their overall returns over the long term.

Of course, like any investment strategy, dollar-cost averaging has its limitations and may not be suitable for everyone. It is important to carefully consider your individual investment goals, risk tolerance, and financial situation before implementing a regular investment plan.

For those who do choose to invest regularly, there are several practical steps that can help maximize the benefits of this approach. Here are a few tips to keep in mind:

1. Automate your investments: One of the easiest ways to ensure consistency in your investing is to automate the process. Many brokerage firms and investment platforms offer tools that allow you to set up automatic contributions to your investment accounts, which can help you stay on track and avoid the temptation to skip a month or make an impulsive decision.

2. Set realistic goals: Before setting up a regular investment plan, take some time to define your financial goals and determine how much you can realistically afford to invest on a regular basis. Be sure to factor in any other expenses or financial obligations you may have, and aim to strike a balance between investing regularly and maintaining a comfortable lifestyle.

3. Choose the right index fund: As we discussed earlier, choosing the right index fund is a critical component of Buffett's index fund strategy. Look for funds with low expense ratios and fees, and consider factors like diversification and historical performance when making your selection.

4. Rebalance your portfolio periodically: Over time, your portfolio may become unbalanced due to market fluctuations. Rebalancing your portfolio helps you maintain your target allocation, manage risk, and capitalize on opportunities.

5. Stay the course: Long-term investing requires patience and discipline. Avoid the temptation to react to short-term market fluctuations and stick to your investment plan. Remember, compounding takes time, but it can have a powerful effect on your wealth over the long term.

By investing regularly and consistently in low-cost index funds, individual investors can take advantage of the power of compounding and build wealth over time. While the strategy may not offer the excitement or allure of active trading or investing in individual stocks, it has proven to be a reliable and effective way to achieve long-term financial goals while minimizing risk and maximizing returns.

# CHAPTER FOUR: BALANCE

Rebalancing your index fund portfolio is an essential aspect of Warren Buffet's investment strategy. Market fluctuations can cause your portfolio to become unbalanced, resulting in a deviation from your original asset allocation. Over time, some assets may grow faster than others, causing your portfolio to become overweight in those areas. Rebalancing helps you maintain your target allocation, manage risk, and capitalize on opportunities.

## What is rebalancing?

Rebalancing involves adjusting your portfolio to bring it back to its original asset allocation. For example, suppose your original target asset allocation was 60% stocks and 40% bonds. If your stock investments grew faster than your bond investments, your portfolio could become unbalanced, with a higher percentage of stocks and a lower percentage of bonds. Rebalancing would involve selling some of your stock investments and buying more bonds to bring your portfolio back to its original asset allocation.

## Why is rebalancing important?

Rebalancing your portfolio is crucial because it helps you manage risk and stay on track to meet your financial goals. A well-diversified portfolio is one of the best ways to manage risk, but a lack of diversification can leave you vulnerable to market volatility. By rebalancing, you ensure that your portfolio remains diversified and aligned with your investment goals.

Rebalancing also helps you capitalize on opportunities in the market. As you sell assets that have grown in value and buy those that have underperformed, you are essentially buying low and selling high. This approach can help you maximize your returns over the long term.

### When should you rebalance your index fund portfolio?

There is no one-size-fits-all answer to this question, as the optimal rebalancing frequency will depend on your investment goals, risk tolerance, and time horizon. Some investors prefer to rebalance their portfolio quarterly or annually, while others may opt for a more infrequent rebalancing schedule.

One common approach is to rebalance when your portfolio deviates from your target allocation by a certain percentage. For example, you might choose to rebalance when your portfolio is more than 5% off your target allocation. This approach allows you to avoid the need for constant monitoring of your portfolio while still ensuring that it remains aligned with your investment goals.

### How to rebalance your index fund portfolio

Rebalancing your index fund portfolio is a straightforward process. Here are the basic steps:

1. Review your portfolio: Start by reviewing your current portfolio and determining how it has changed since you last rebalanced.

2. Determine your target allocation: Decide on your desired asset allocation based on your financial goals, risk tolerance, and time horizon.

3. Calculate the necessary trades: Determine the trades necessary to bring your portfolio back to your target allocation. This may involve selling some assets that have grown in value and buying those that have underperformed.

4. Execute the trades: Place your trades to adjust your portfolio back to your target allocation.

5. Monitor your portfolio: Keep an eye on your portfolio to ensure that it remains aligned with your investment goals, and rebalance as necessary.

Rebalancing your index fund portfolio is an essential aspect of Warren Buffet's investment strategy. It helps you maintain your target allocation, manage risk, and capitalize on opportunities in the market. By following a regular rebalancing schedule, you can ensure that your portfolio remains diversified and aligned with your financial goals. Remember, consistency is key to long-term wealth building, and rebalancing is just one of the many tools you can use to stay on track.

Stay the course: Long-term index fund investing requires patience and discipline. Avoid the temptation to react to short-term market fluctuations and stick to your investment plan. Remember, compounding takes time, but it can have a powerful effect on your wealth over the long term.

# CHAPTER FIVE: DISCIPLINE

This final step of Warren Buffett's index fund strategy is perhaps the most important of all. Investing is not a get-rich-quick scheme, and the most successful investors are often those who can maintain their discipline and avoid making impulsive decisions. Market volatility is a fact of life, and it can be tempting to try to time the market or react to short-term fluctuations. However, research has shown time and time again that attempting to time the market is a losing strategy in the long run. The best way to invest in the market is to buy and hold a diversified portfolio of low-cost index funds and let the power of compounding work its magic over time.

In the short term, the stock market can be incredibly unpredictable. It's not uncommon for stock prices to rise or fall by several percentage points in a single day, and these fluctuations can be driven by a wide range of factors, from global events to company-specific news. However, over the long term, the stock market tends to be much more predictable, and the direction of the market is driven by fundamental economic factors like corporate earnings, interest rates, and inflation.

By staying the course and avoiding the temptation to react to short-term fluctuations, you can take advantage of the long-term growth potential of the stock market. Over time, the stock market has historically delivered an average annual return of around 10%, which means that if you invest in a low-cost index fund and hold it for the long term, you can expect to earn returns that will compound over time and potentially grow into a substantial nest egg.

The key to staying the course is to have a long-term perspective and to focus on the fundamentals of the companies that you are invested in. While short-term fluctuations can be unsettling, over the long term, the stock market tends to follow the underlying economic trends, and successful investors are those who can remain patient and avoid making impulsive decisions based on short-term market movements.

## Conclusion

Warren Buffett's index fund strategy is a time-tested approach to long-term investing that has helped countless investors build wealth over time. By starting with a sound investment plan, choosing low-cost index funds, investing regularly, rebalancing your portfolio periodically, and staying the course, you can take advantage of the power of compounding and potentially grow your wealth over the long term. While there are no guarantees in investing, the historical performance of the stock market suggests that a disciplined, long-term approach is likely to be the most successful over time.

In conclusion, Warren Buffet's index fund strategy is based on a simple but powerful philosophy: invest in low-cost index funds over the long term and stick to a sound investment plan. Buffet's approach is based on the principles of value investing, which emphasizes buying high-quality companies at a reasonable price. By following Buffet's 5-step approach, investors can benefit from the long-term compounding effect of index fund investing. A sound investment plan tailored to individual goals, risk tolerance, and time horizon is crucial to staying on track during market volatility. Choosing a low-cost index fund, such as an S&P 500 fund, offers broad exposure to the market and diversification.

Consistently investing a set amount each month or quarter allows for dollar-cost averaging, smoothing the impact of market fluctuations on your portfolio. Rebalancing your portfolio periodically helps maintain a target allocation, manage risk, and capitalize on opportunities.

Staying the course and avoiding reacting to short-term market fluctuations is key to long-term success. Patience and discipline are essential to reap the benefits of compounding over time.

In summary, Warren Buffet's index fund strategy provides a straightforward and effective way to build wealth over the long term. By implementing these 5 steps, investors can enjoy the benefits of a low-cost, diversified, and passive investment approach that has a proven track record of success.